MW01268292

expectantseed
the essence of Jesus

Bill Rinehart

[signature]

PRESS

TABLE OF CONTENTS

don't read this book...

in any particular order, unless you really, really want to. I decided not to string the chapters together. They all stand alone. Some read like emails because that is how they began. Some are very short and others not so short.

This book is a compilation of two years of conversations with God and my church family. At times, you will look over the shoulder of one of my friends and read their electronic devotion. I could have edited the structure but chose not to. By the way, the friend who copy-edited this manuscript, Molly Owen, protested about that. It's not her fault. She is a proofing genius.

I hope just one thing touches you as profoundly as all of it has touched me. If it does, then email me and we will continue the conversation.

bill@unitedassembly.com

special seed

Cindy, Bear, Bo and Hannah have always been seed and deserve chapters of their own. They write them with their lives every day.

Bo knows design. My son's fingerprints are on the cover and all over my life. His sketching of the little girl inside has been an inspiration to thousands of people.

Chris Owen assisted with design and truly deserves to share the author credit for his ideas, thousands of hours as a sounding board and his technical genius.

The family at UAG provides constant models of the truth of this book.

Molly Owen fixed my grammar and found my errors. From verb tenses to run-on sentences and awkward wording, she helped me with sensitivity and brilliance. She identified the things that would make me look foolish and helped me keep my voice in the text.

by the way...this is a seed:

Jesus' secret essence

It is not really a secret. It's more like a mystery, in a New Testament kind of way. It is such a profoundly simple principle that it cannot really be true, can it? There is no doubt that it is counter-cultural and defies all contemporary logic. *Yet, to embrace it unleashes the most potent of God's promises and the most liberating of His laws.* I'm talking about the power of a seed.

I recently awoke from a sound sleep just before the sun rose. I'm not an early morning person and usually drink two cups of coffee and stare at the wall for thirty minutes before I can construct a lucid thought. But on this morning I felt that God was speaking something profound to me. Even now, as I write these pages, its power and simplicity excite and propel me toward the ultimate destiny for my life… the same as yours, by the way. I clearly sensed that "God assigns inestimable value to those who realize their value as seed." This awkward phrase (try saying "inestimable" three times fast) has clarified several of God's "mysteries" and "secrets."

I believe that two things hamper our appreciation of this truth. Most of us are several generations removed from our agrarian roots. I do all my harvesting at the grocery store; my hunting and fishing as well, incidentally. In addition to that, there was an abuse of this spiritual law in the '70s and '80s by those who desperately needed to fund the machinery of high-powered, media-driven ministry. Fearing that I might not get you past the cover, I hesitated about using the word "seed" in the title.

If you will only capture the following idea; that God has determined that SEED is _precious_ (Psalm 126:6, KJV), that _sacrifice_ is the noble destiny for every SEED, and that the shining moment for every SEED is _harvest,_ then even this brief introduction will have had some impact.

We are called to shine, to manifest the Glory of God. Isaiah's prophecy for God's people remains ours to be realized. A dark world awaits the impact of a believer who knows that he or she is most fulfilled as seed. Every harvest begins with seed.

the million dollar rabbit

I am a debtor to church camp. The moments of emotional and spiritual upheaval that led to my ministry call, my mission's world-view, and the formation of my life message occurred at one week or another of summer camp. As an adult, I became the state youth director for my denomination and provided programs for thousands of kids spanning eight years. One week each summer, we sponsored a free camp for kids who had been removed from their homes for reasons of abuse or neglect.

You couldn't miss the purple bunny rabbit. The little girl held it tightly against her chest as she stood in line to check in. The rabbit stood out because it was all she brought. The usual pillow, bedroll and suitcase were missing. Neat corn-rows, braided with bright pink beads ran from her forehead to the nape of her neck. Neat as a pin. Cute as a button. Someone had tenderly prepared her, although she was woefully under-equipped for five days away from home.

Her story wasn't markedly worse or better than her cabin mates. She had been infected with genital herpes by her father. She was nine years old. I know these things because of the bunny rabbit. Her foster care family knew that we had a concession stand, and that we would allow children to deposit money in our camp "bank" upon arrival. Ice cream, candy and soft drinks could be debited from the balance on deposit. I had been amazed at the disposable income some of these campers carried around. It wasn't unusual for a child to bring a check for $50 or more, enough to bring on a diabetic coma with candy bars. Her little bank held $1.28.

You have to hand it to those special people who take in these little victims. Along with safe haven, three squares and a decent place to sleep, someone was also trying to impart a lesson on thrift. To that end, a cast-off plastic "Easter Bunny" was recycled after having dispensed its jelly beans, or whatever. The removable head had been taped on and a quarter-sized slit had been crudely cut out of its back. The figure was jammed with pennies, mostly, and this she extended to us without hesitation.

Among our church family we have an expression that describes the instant that some great truth breaks upon us. My friend, Pastor Chris Owen, calls these experiences, "God moments." Something gels. We get it. The awakening is palpable and evident on the face of the receiver. My "God moment" with this little girl would linger until now, even deepening with fresh revelation as I think of it. She trusted us completely. She surrendered her treasure entirely, and it would pay huge dividends.

She hit the jackpot. Won the lottery. Publisher's Clearing House drove up to her door with a huge check. Had these things actually happened, it could not have seemed any better for her. I had a week and all she had in the world -- $1.28. For the next few days, she withdrew from a bottomless account. I am sure that she never stopped to think about it, never stopped to do the math. She just ate when she was hungry and drank when she was thirsty and the goodies just kept coming. More than fifteen years later, I am still thrilled at the thought that I was able to be her benefactor.

It happens every Sunday at our church. The single mom, the elderly couple, and the college student all extend to the Father resources it seems they can ill-afford to give up. And every Sunday, the Father sees them the way I saw the little girl with the bunny. "What can I do to bless them?" he responds; and the windows of heaven fly open to disgorge their treasure…finance and time and blessing…purpose and promise and power…family and friends and familiarity in the Kingdom. *HOW* He does it is simple. Like me, as director of the camp, He has the _authority_ and He has the _resources_. *WHY* he does it will become evident in the following pages.

Just as it did for me, when I held in my hands the purple bunny rabbit bank, the innocence, trust, and obedience _touches His heart._ As long as I was in charge, this little one would be supplied. Had she asked for anything, I would have exhausted all funds to provide it. It would be worth it because I truly believe that the _potential yield_ from her initial dollar and twenty-eight cents may indeed reach into the millions. What might happen, if you and others who read her story were urged to trust God with a few more resources, and a little more time? What might happen if we pass the story along, if we "pay it forward" as the hit movie suggests? I believe that to know the answer will ultimately reveal the "secret of the harvest." So simple, and yet so profound that it could change the world forever.

tsunami and the seed boat

My kids will tell you that about the time they reached middle-school, their dad left "cool" in the rear view mirror. I was proud of the purchase of the plastic sandals. They were the color of sand and were imprinted with a leather-like pattern. Only eight bucks! High fashion, as long as I didn't wear black knee-high socks on my glow-in-the dark legs, right? I felt the anguish in my younger son's voice. "Where did you get those, Dad?" I proudly told him that I had gotten them at the drug store, to which he whined, "Did anyone SEE you buy them?"

It wasn't the first or last time that I would commit such a grievous fashion mistake that would cause them to want to crawl in a hole and die. I can only imagine what Noah's boys discussed as their father constructed the barge in the back yard. I wonder how that went down when it came up in conversation with their peers. It must not have been *too* difficult explaining why their dad was building an ocean liner in the middle of the Turkish desert. The world's first theme park, right? Carpet golf on the upper-deck. A couple of fish and chips kiosks. "Come spend a weekend with us and bring your pets."

And how would the brothers discuss it among themselves? "What is dad thinking? It hasn't rained in our lifetime. We are hundreds of miles from the nearest beach. How are we going to tow it to the water? *This is our inheritance.*"

And every man who has ever "reasoned" with his wife about the absolute necessity of a satellite system or a hunting rifle can appreciate the fact that Sister Noah (Joan of Ark) may have had a few comments on the wisdom of such an enterprise. Can you hear the pillow talk? "It's really looking great, dear, but don't you think that you are a little *overboard* (sorry) on this project?" The scripture doesn't tell us that God laid it all out for the lady. Apparently, only Noah got the call. And he only got it once. That was enough. From that time on, all he had and was became seed.

Do you suppose that God could find a man, or a woman, like that in this generation? Would He even bother to look? The question has never made more sense: "When the Son of Man comes, will he find faith on the earth?" (*Luke 18:8*) Do His eyes still search out the person whose "heart is pure toward Him?" (*2 Chronicles 16:9*) What hope does this culture have without a Noah? *At least in his day, they had a chance.* There was someone for whom compassion for his neighbors' condition outweighed his concern about their comments. The Bible tells us that they blew it off -- right up until the day Noah entered the Ark. *Do we exhibit enough faith that men would call it folly?*

Most probably thought he was a "few fries short of a Happy Meal," a Don Quixote-esque fool on a fool's mission. Rain? Right. Next, you're going to tell me that a fictional divine is going to visit judgement on the earth again. It never rains here, not on our parade. All we need to know about the weather, or whether or not there is a God, we can learn from the web, right? Does anybody really sense an urgency to protect his family from the effects of the culture, to the extent that we make the church the center of our lives? All of that was for generations long ago and far away…like scenes from a scratchy, old, black and white movie.

Fruitcake? Religious relic? You have to grant him this much. He worked and he witnessed. He whittled and he warned. He could live with the ridicule. He couldn't live with a generation on his conscience. Go ahead and laugh. Undaunted, Noah preached to them. "There is room for you and you are welcome aboard. Please don't play fast and loose with your life, with your family. Please."

Noah's faith compelled him to be that which God values most -- a seed. He died the death of pride. He invested rather than consumed. This was not the by-product of a woodworking hobby. It was an obsession. His sacrifice was total. He finished it, too, by the way. No half-built boat up on blocks in the desert. No haunting reminders of best intentions gone by the way. He finished the thing and she floated.

What else can one do when he or she realizes that lost means lost and when God shuts the door, all who are on the outside are done? Who would not build, whether it be a literal or metaphorical ark to the saving of his family? Which of us is beyond the responsibility of going, doing, giving, and saying what is necessary to communicate the availability of grace and deliverance?

Forget the engineering. One and a half football fields long. Seventy-five feet wide and nearly five stories tall. Forget the logistics -- that's a lot of lumber. Forget how labor intensive it must have been. *Four guys and no power tools.* As amazing as all this, Noah probably funded the whole deal. That means that along with his reputation, he invested all he had, and his entire future, on a word from God about impending judgement. The world would not see compassion again like that until Jesus. Indeed, Peter's first letter tells us that the Spirit of Jesus patiently preached through Noah, offering an ark of safety. In the end, there were only eight takers. Incredible.

Then it happened. Tsunami. The Genesis account includes "all the springs of the great deep." The rains came down and the flood came up. The images of the devastation of January 2005 are still fresh. One hundred fifty thousand people died in a massive surge of water in Southern Asia. Did it happen like that? It must have been sudden and without warning, or else it is logical to assume that some could at least have bundled a few sticks together in a makeshift raft.

In the six hundredth year of Noah's life, on the seventeenth day of the second month—on that day all the springs of the great deep burst forth, and the floodgates of the heavens were opened. And rain fell on the earth forty days and forty nights. (Genesis 7:11-12)

We don't know if Noah grieved for those outside the door when God shut it. We don't know if he heard the screams of the dying, or the cries of the children who naively trusted mom and dad with their safety. We can't know how frustrated he must have felt at the tragic waste. It didn't have to be this way.

Many have found humor in the story of Noah. Have you ever traveled with a pet? Imagine what dinner time was like. Did the animals eat their way down the food chain? Is it possible that God herded two of every species of animal onto the boat in the same amount of time that it took four women to pack? Somebody crack a window, I think the Rhino ate something bad! By the way, be careful where you step. Don't eat yellow...ANYTHING! Some have speculated that conversation was difficult over the chatter of the monkeys, lowing of the cattle, and roar of the felines.

One thing I know. If and when it ever got quiet, if the population of the zoo decks were ever rocked to sleep by the pitch and yaw of the ark, if Noah ever listened to the water lapping against the sides of the vessel as he sank into sleep...he was never troubled by the background noise of a troubled conscience. No regrets. He had been a fool for God...a fool declaring that hope floats. His family lived to tell about it. And all of us who have ridden an ark of safety to this point owe so much to the little old ladies who foolishly skirmished in prayer until the sun came up. We are in debt to the preachers who dotted the landscape with little missions, dedicated to the saving of their "families" from judgement. Fools like us understand that, **"He is no fool who gives what he cannot keep to gain what he cannot lose." --Jim Eliott**

Indeed, you are no fool if you understand that *God assigns inestimable value to those who recognize their value as seed.* It is the secret of the harvest. In the midst of a world that must increasingly test the limits of God's grace...

The LORD saw how great man's wickedness on the earth had become, and that every inclination of the thoughts of his heart was only evil all the time.

The LORD was grieved that he had made man on the earth, and his heart was filled with pain. So the LORD said, "I will wipe mankind, whom I have created, from the face of the earth—men and animals, and creatures that move along the ground, and birds of the air—for I am grieved that I have made them." (Genesis 6:6-7)

…and

As it was in the days of Noah, so it will be at the coming of the Son of Man… (Matthew 24:37)

In the middle of this mess, if God can find a Noah who, motivated by a holy fear for the casualties of impending judgment, will forsake his own comfort and invest himself in the saving of the family, perhaps he too will know the favor of God. Perhaps, before the final Tsunami of judgment, God will once more validate the investment of the seed with harvest, rather than holocaust.

the need for seed

Every harvest begins with seed.

There is a built-in hesitation about discussing seed with God's people. Pastors presume that there is a great resistance to any mention of money and with good reason. Many have suffered the effects of every charlatan and dealer in indulgences who has exercised their greed at the expense of good people. It's true enough, that there are mercenary and unprincipled people who have taken advantage of those least able to fund the lavish lifestyles of the religious rich and famous.

I carry all this baggage with me in a yearly treatment of the subject, which I approach in an almost apologetic and fearful manner. It just isn't right. Why should we have to back into a consideration about supporting God's work with hat in hand and a boat load of disclaimers? It is obvious which kingdom gains from a reluctance to discuss the need for financial support. It isn't right, when every product and pitch-man assails us from every square inch of blank space on hats, race cars, and stadium walls. Hawking everything from aspirin to Viagra, the media assails us from the television screen every seven minutes, from three to four minutes at a time, trying to separate a fool and his money. Those of us who do in fact feed and clothe the marginalized are made to feel guilty for seeking the money it takes to drive benevolent efforts.

And then consider the fact, that in this most blessed of all nations, there is a multi-million dollar market niche for pet psychiatry and animal plastic surgery. Don't talk about money in church, but get Sparky some breast enhancement, lest she suffer from a low sense of self-esteem. Ridiculous, but reality nonetheless. It occurs to me now, that some may have bailed on this book, having sensed that we have moved from anecdote to application. I guess it is the paranoia.

Being sensitive about this issue, I began our yearly focus on finance by giving our church a literal "hand." I had found a molded plexi-glas massager that could be held in the palm of one's hand. I bought several hundred and our ushers distributed them at the onset of the message to our amused parishioners. "Turn to your neighbor," I began, "and massage him or her between the shoulder blades." Having said this, I acknowledged the tension that is created when preaching about money. Only then, did I feel that people were disarmed enough to hear something fresh about seed.

It is a rather narrow understanding of seed to

think of it only as money. It is anything that we value, really. It could be time or energy, passion or compassion. What is more significant is the fact that seed is not just something that we give, but that we can be! The Apostle Paul, in his second letter to converts at Corinth, wrote, "I will very gladly spend for you everything I have and expend myself as well." It is possible to spend and to be spent. Until we are spent, we cannot say we have done all that we can do. To acknowledge that having exhausted all my resources, I yet have something to contribute is a huge responsibility. To know that there is something that we withhold has clearly revealed our priorities. This knowledge brings great responsibility. Denying is easier than complying, I guess. No doubt, sowing seed is expensive. *Being seed is fatal.*

Just ask Jesus. The subheading in John 12 reads,

> "Jesus Predicts His Death"

Now there were some Greeks among those who went up to worship at the Feast. They came to Philip, who was from Bethsaida in Galilee, with a request. "Sir," they said, "we would like to see Jesus." (John 12:20-21)

What do you think they were after? It was the celebration of the Feast of Passover...the last one under the old covenant. Jerusalem was the destination for the faithful throughout the world and they came seeking...*what?* Do you think that any of them expected a face to face with God? Could it be that most people simply acted out of a sense of obligation? Tradition? Guilt? What was accomplished by making the trek and visiting Israel's most sacred site? Is there anything redemptive about traveling to headquarters for the denomination?

They couldn't have known how significant their journey could be. We have to believe, though, that HE IS THE REWARDER of those who seek Him diligently. There is no question that these seekers were rewarded. As ignorant of the portent as they may have been, they had an incredibly intimate revelation of who Jesus was and what He was ultimately all about.

I wonder when it dawned on them. Was there an epiphany as they observed Calvary from a distance? Do you think that they were spiritually keen enough to discern the meaning in His cryptic words? The power and majesty of His declaration are evident to us now. But did *THEY* get it? Sadly, most of the church world does not yet "get it." Still self-serving, easily distracted and shortsighted. Can we learn from them the wisdom and reward of seeking an encounter with Him? Isn't every lesson, every scripture, every shoulder rub with God's people an aspect of God's attributes waiting to be revealed? Doesn't He, in fact, yearn to reveal Himself in sensitive detail to those who move beyond casual observation? AND, if this is true, haven't we wasted enough life wading in the shallows of His presence when we could plumb the depths of the Son of God?

Jesus had entered the city facing a wild and enthusiastic crowd, proclaiming Him King of Israel, inflaming both the Pharisees and their cruel masters, the Romans. It is likely that word of the miracles, not the least of which was the raising of Lazarus from the dead, had traveled to Greece and beyond. Jesus, the Lamb of God, was about to be slain for the sins of the world. This context allows me to be generous with our reading of this encounter. It is absolutely loaded with significance. Think about it. Lazarus lives. Gentiles are inquiring about Jesus. His disciples are facilitating introduction. HE GIVES A METAPHOR ABOUT SEED!

Curious, the pilgrims request an audience with the teacher. Philip, concerned with protocol, runs this one past Andrew, who was comfortable introducing anybody to the Master.

Philip went to tell Andrew; Andrew and Philip in turn told Jesus. (John 12:22)

Obviously, Jesus was accommodating and gracious. He gave them so much more than they had asked for. They asked for a meeting; He bore His soul. His response to them revealed the man, the message, and the mission.

Jesus replied, "The hour has come for the Son of Man to be glorified. I tell you the truth, unless a kernel of wheat falls to the ground and dies, it remains only a single seed. But if it dies, it produces many seeds." (John 12:23-24)

As far as I know, we never hear from these Greeks again. It's possible that they only wanted to see what all the fuss was about. Perhaps they had a kind of fascination with celebrity, and Jesus was certainly that. They might have had the shallowest of all motivations for desiring to meet Him. Jesus' response, however, seems directed to all who would seek to know Him intimately. His discourse not only reveals the regenerative power of the seed, it uncovers the secret of harvest and exposes the very heart of God. There is first the need for seed. Every harvest begins with seed.

God assigns inestimable value to those who realize their value as seed.

I woke up one morning with this sentence on my mind. I couldn't shake it. I couldn't force it back down into the neverland of sleep. It apprehended and arrested me. God assigns value, great value, to those who aspire to be seed? I can't imagine a more important quest than to know what God values. Some of us are beginning to appreciate that somebody has switched the price tags around in our culture.

Heaven's economy has a greatly diminished valuation on gold, for example. That which has inflamed the greed of kings and driven conquest and wars paves celestial parking lots. Virtue is of greater worth by far, and that from one of history's wealthiest monarchs, King Solomon. A good name, credibility and integrity are exceedingly more valuable than any currency. The first shall be last...the greatest among you is the servant of all...and on it goes.

To the farmer, seed is security. It is the means to harvest and harvest feeds his family. The seed is precious because he relies on it. As a metaphor, seed represents anything that we might lean on for support. I've heard all of my life that the institutions we trust may need to crumble if we are ever going to trust God and seek Him first. Our hope does not rest in a strong economy. Our hope cannot rest in our political systems. Economics and politics have failed many times, and with the failures, men's hearts fail for fear. When we let go of whatever we are trusting more than God, we begin to discover the dimension of "beyond all we could ask or even imagine."

You have to let go of the seed. You have to relinquish all control and resist the urge to hang on to, or save, or consume the seed. This is especially hard if you are convinced that you need the seed to survive. An elder in my church, Ronnie, made a great observation one evening in my office. "Sometimes the seed looks a lot like a meal." No question about it. If times are hard and prospects are slim and seed corn will fill the space in your stomach, who wouldn't consider eating the seed? You gotta eat, right? How hard it is sometimes to release the seed into the ground. Yet, failing to do so severely limits the power of the seed. *It's nacho seed!*

There are several aspects of this that I will cover in the pages that follow. There are so many well-worn truisms about seed. But for this moment, whoever you are that God hit my "pause" button for, what follows may be for your affirmation, confirmation, or even direction.

Jesus said the seed must fall into the ground and die. The NIV says that otherwise, it remains a single seed. The King James Version says it a little differently.

Verily, verily, I say unto you, Except a corn of wheat fall into the ground and die, <u>it abideth alone</u>: but if it die, it bringeth forth much fruit. (John 12:24) (emphasis mine)

"It abideth alone..." The Elizabethan translators have caused the idea to be imprinted in my mind. What does that mean? Doesn't the seed die anyway? Indeed, EVERY SEED IS DESTINED TO DIE. Left alone, a seed will die in the bag on the porch. SEED HAS AN EXPIRATION DATE, a shelf-life. Its intent is to be planted, INVESTED, to be sown into the ground and die. OTHERWISE, it simply gets too old to produce fruit. I know it is true. I have sown grass seed that languished under my house for years and nothing came up.

It abideth alone -- language describing a missed

opportunity -- the personal description for people populating "Someday Isle."

It abideth alone. My greatest fear is to live an insignificant life. There is a window of opportunity that is only open for a moment. It has taken a tragically long time to wake up and realize that my greatest value is as a seed. So late, but not too late.

I don't know what my lasting contribution will be. I only know that I aspire to be at least this much like Jesus. He relinquished all his rights, placing Himself in the Father's hands, pocket change to be spent on the harvest. "Not MY will," He said.

Matt Redmond wrote a powerful song:

Blessed be your name, when the sun is shining down on me... When the world's all that it should be, blessed be your name
Blessed be your name on the road marked with suffering... Though there's pain in the offering
Blessed be your name

You give and take away...
My heart will choose to say, Lord blessed be your name.

It is truly not your seed.

On day 37 of our 40-day email series on seed, I wrote about the miracle when Aaron's staff sprouted almond bearing shoots.

The miracle was God's response to rebellion against authority and retained a vital lesson for those *in a place of authority as well. Make no mistake. The principle of spiritual authority is one of God's core values. He will vindicate those He has placed in leadership with fruitfulness and effectiveness.*

The seeds of rebellion were first sown in Eden and have borne fruit in every generation since then. It is a part of our spiritual DNA. We must acknowledge it and wage a personal war against it. To deny it only affirms that we are enslaved by it. "I confess it, Lord. It is me, standing in the need of prayer." *Stop right here and pray it. "Father, open my eyes to the reality of my own rebellion. Grieve me with it, as it must grieve You until I can truly put my will to death."*

Now Moses was a remarkable man. Like you and me, he wrestled with his limitations in the face of growing responsibility and radical change. There was once a time though, when he didn't have anything to prove. He was raised in Pharoah's house. He had it all, including the trappings of royalty. But he left it all, CHOOS-ING, the Bible says, to be mistreated along with his enslaved kinsmen over the pleasures of the Egyptian palace. He traded the *scepter of a prince* for the *staff* (walking stick) *of a sheep herder.* It is that staff I want you to consider because you have one as well. You, like Moses, Aaron, me and everyone else have something that we lean on. Something props us up and, as long as we insist on holding it, we have some measure of rebellion to contend with.

In Moses' case, it was a poor man's scepter. In Exodus 4, we begin to see the role this staff will play at the burning bush.

Then the Lord said to him, "What is that in your hand?" "A staff," he replied. The Lord said, "THROW IT ON THE GROUND." (Exodus 4:2-3)

We need to live in the text for a minute. Think of the elements that make up this event. There is a burning bush that doesn't burn up. The audible voice of God calls Moses *by name.* Think about it. We are talking God here. "I AM" calls and commissions the man who forty years earlier had lashed out in retribution, killing a man and turning the "Prince of Egypt" into the keeper of his father-in-law's sheep. NOW he is to lead the Hebrews out from more than four hundred years of bondage. Six hundred thousand people whose great, great, grandmothers had only heard stories about freedom are now following the guy who had been living in a tent for forty years.

Let's do a quick inventory of the things Moses brings to the table. Let's see... He has a stick and a stutter. Oh yeah, he also has a criminal record. Sounds like leadership material to me. But don't miss the importance of those two verses above. *There was only one thing that gave him a measure of comfort.* Like every Bedouin macho man, he has a STAFF baby. He could fight off small varmints with the thing. History tells us that royals carry scepters, but you and I carry staffs. The original Hebrew word for staff means a symbol of authority. In our context, it represents our personal fiefdoms--the little kingdoms where we hold court with those who are unfortunate enough to have a somewhat lesser status. You get this, don't you? STAFFers are everywhere. Find the least educated, skilled and talented people in unskilled jobs *and let them supervise one person, or guard the dumpster, or man the gate.* It won't take long to see how desperately people will cling to that staff. *If you want MY staff, you can pry it out of my cold, clammy, dead fingers.*

But God said to Moses, "Throw it on the ground," and when he let it go, the miracles started to happen.

Captain Kirk was wrong. Space is not the "final frontier." For most of us, the last virgin territory is *submission*. The prefix *sub* means "*under or beneath*." Mission is what we were born and then born again to do in life. The *mission* defines us, **not the staff**. Our offices or titles mean little to anyone except ourselves. The truth is, you can be the "King of Nothing." And that is where many of us will end up. The record shows, they took the blows and did it... well, they blew it actually. Remember that haunting little phrase, "it abideth alone"? The pull to be a big fish in a little pond is so great. We just *have* to control the staff (the seed). Having never been willing to die the death of a seed, many of us will never know about baskets and barns bursting with the favor of God. Independent? No one fences you in? Think you're unique? Enjoy it. This moment is all there is for you. Do you think you ought to let go of the staff now?

Just ask a guy named Korah. We are in Numbers, chapter 16. His story is disturbingly familiar. The centuries and the names have changed but the story line is common. You may think you are the author of your own script, but if you are in rebellion, you are no more in control of your destiny than Grandma is after a dose of salt.

Korah, son of Izhar, the son of Kohath, the son of Levi, and certain Reubenites—Dathan and Abiram, sons of Eliab, and On, son of Peleth—became insolent and rose up against Moses. With them were 250 Israelite men, well-known community leaders who had been appointed members of the council. They came as a group to oppose Moses and Aaron and said to them, "You have gone too far! The whole community is holy, every one of them, and the LORD is with them. Why then do you set yourselves above the LORD'S assembly?" (Numbers 16:1-3)

I know Korah rather well. I've BEEN Korah. I've

been infected with the same virus that infected Adam and has been passed to all of us. Which of us has not resisted authority? Which of us has not been smarter than the person in the next higher position? "Who does he think he is?" We've all said that. "The whole community is holy..." Let me interpret that spirit in our context. "I don't need a program, a church, or Godly counsel... they are just men like the rest of us." Read on.

In a dramatic showdown, God asks of Aaron what he had already asked of Moses years earlier--to lay down the symbol of his leadership and authority. The rebels were humiliated and God brought life through a lifeless stick.

It's nacho seed. So let go of it. It is about giving up our lives and resources to the mission. It is about letting go of those things He asks of us. Not my will, but yours, Lord. Amazing things can happen through a Moses or an Aaron if he will lay...if YOU will lay down your staff. Miracles and plagues and passage and provision-- God wants to work incredible things through the resources He places in our hands IF we won't hold them too tightly. Upon reading Numbers 17, you'll find that Korah receives judgement as God places his stamp of approval upon a man who was willing to lay down the same staff that he had bested a Pharoah with. Aaron's staff, abandoned at the altar where Moses met with God, BUDDED.

Do YOU want to bear fruit? Is it all about harvest--the mission--for you? I guess we will see. I recently asked that of my young ministry team. We went around the room and named those things which were precious to each of them: the youth ministry, preaching, technology, every little kingdom we presided over. All of them--Chris, Jimmy, Natalie, Stephen, Jill, Joyce and Matt--lay down their ministry needs and budgets so that we could funnel all possible resources toward the building of our school in Colombia. These precious people became precious seed and declared that the MISSION was their priority.

The sound of staffs hitting the floor must have sounded like thunder in the bowels of hell.

One last thought. Great things can be done with a loosely held staff. Great harm can be done when we abuse what God has given. Moses got water from a rock on two different occasions. The first time, according to God's instruction, he struck the rock and life-giving water gushed out. Later, in a similar incident, God gave different instructions. By this time, Moses had gotten quite good with the staff. He leaned on it quite a bit. He got his swagger from it. Ignoring God's wishes, he struck the rock again. Hey. It worked the first time right? But once more, God wanted to see if Moses would be willing to lay it down and trust Him. He was not, and paid a dear price. When you lay it down, it becomes seed.

jimmy the seed

The inspiration for this chapter walked into my office late one afternoon. You cannot imagine what a thrill it is to have someone with whom I have covenanted to change the world share with me his passion to be seed.

Pastor Jimmy is a miracle. He wasn't reared in a Christian home, and yet, thrived through Bible college, married a wonderful girl from a "churched" background and is now the proud father of Julia and Taylor James. In addition to all of that, he is pastoring one of the most dynamic youth groups in our state. He is God's gift to this generation of young people, and we could not be more blessed.

His humility in my office struck me that day. He had emailed me earlier in the week about what I thought God might be doing in him. What was the next level? How could I become seed? His heart beat for missions. Was he supposed to be a missionary? *He's there, I thought. He gets it!* No question about it. I told him so. If only all of us could say like the psalmist, Kelly Carpenter whose lyrics we have sung, "I'd lay it all down again, just to hear you say that I'm your friend." Yep, he's there.

I have twenty-five more years of elapsed time

in ministry; yet, I'm not so far ahead of him, if at all, in spiritual maturity. As we spoke that day of his concerns, I rejoiced at the opportunity to sow a little seed in such good ground. "The key is letting it go," I said…again. The two hardest things about seed are the desire to consume it and the need to control it. If we insist, God will let us keep the seed. But then it abides alone. *Whatever nourishment it gives for the moment is all that there will be.* Let it go. Take your hands off that _____(you know what goes here).

IT IS NOT YOURS TO DESIGNATE.

Think on this haunting declaration by an unknown source. "Some people lose their lives by dying; others by wasting their time."

Another thing to consider: There are ten times as many people reading this (at the first press run) than there were in the upper room at Pentecost. They changed the world. As we spend these moments together and speak of "seed," you have to wonder what might happen if we can get on the same page and in the same place.

I wonder if things are going the way Jimmy planned. I'm not sure. I only know my own experience. It reaches back to 1977 when Cindy and I met. We were on a missions trip in Central America. She felt called to missions and so did I, I thought. I knew that would endear me to her, so yeah, I could be a missionary.

Seriously, at one point in our ministry we offered ourselves to our denomination as missionaries. Although it might have happened, we felt a need to wait…a little. We were in music and youth, and ultimately music and television production. I told many people that I had the perfect job. Music. That was my *life.*

Our next move took us to a "rescue" church, meaning that if somebody didn't rescue it, the property would be sold. Was it hard to leave the music? You can't imagine. We left a church that had seemingly unlimited resources. To a music director, it was heaven. The church had an incredible talent pool and all the gadgets needed to be on the cutting edge in worship and production. This first pastorate was our "wilderness" experience. Cindy and I did everything that was done…preaching, playing, and sweeping up after.

Believe it or not, leaving the rescue church was the hardest thing I've ever done. By the time we left, God had replaced all that we had ever given up and with tremendous upgrades. We found ourselves way out in front of the curve in terms of worship. We had a band and vocals LONG before it became cool. Would I ever know that again? I wrestled and grieved and finally let go.

Still not a missionary.

Cindy's whole family had become missionaries. Heroes of the faith, they were. We had moved to Possum Kingdom, America (I'm not kidding) to direct youth and camp ministry for our state organization. We reared our children the next eight years in rural South Carolina, taking yearly missions trips with 40-50 teens. One of those kids later became my Executive Pastor. While state youth director, I managed to "inspire" over one hundred churches to give $37,000 to "Speed the Light," our youth missions fund.

Still, not a missionary.

I told Jimmy that day that I wished everybody understood the dynamics of seed as well as he did. The harvest is God's responsibility, planting the seed is mine.

What, after all, is Apollos? And what is Paul? Only servants, through whom you came to believe—as the Lord has assigned to each his task. I planted the seed, Apollos watered it, but God made it grow. So neither he who plants nor he who waters is anything, but only God, who makes things grow. (1 Corinthians 3:5-7)

Still, not a missionary.

Fifteen years ago we came to our little town to pastor again. I had just written my first book, *Torchbearer's University.* The folks in my fellowship know it as *All Jesus IS.* We'd had it made at the camp. The kids, my married kids, still miss the camp. It will always be the home they go to in their minds. This rural community, in the eyes of some of my friends, seemed the end of the line, the jumping off place. I still meet some of those guys at conferences around the country and patiently explain where we live in reference to a "real" town. When Cindy and I arrived, this fellowship gave $400 a month to missions. About one-fourth of that was actually given by individuals, the rest underwritten in the budget.

Still, not a missionary.

I just reviewed the Year-to-date report on our giving. The church now underwrites $0, yet people just like YOU, give over $2000 a week to World and Home Missions through our outreach "The Band of Brothers." There is a church that is broadcasting the Gospel to the heart of the Arab world from Amman, Jordan. We furnished the production suite. Pastor Jimmy recently delivered a brand new Toyota to a missionary in South Africa. We have his picture handing over the keys to a $30,000 car that we paid for. Each year, over one hundred people from our fellowship build churches and Bible schools in places like India, Cuba, Costa Rica and Romania. As a result of the first series on "expectantseed," our foreign missionaries had their monthly support from our church DOUBLED, without having to travel back to the

States to ask for it. The Band of Brothers and our youth group gave $60,000 to buy equipment for missionaries in one year, which ranked us number eight of ten thousand churches and catapulted our state to ranking number one in its category.

Still, not a missionary. Just seed.

The Temple Mount in Jerusalem is regarded as the most holy site in the world. Islam's holiest site, The Dome of the Rock, is built over the place where Muslims claim Abraham offered *Ishmael* as a sacrifice, only to see him spared at the last moment. Most of us have a little problem with that. Right place. Wrong son. And over this detail, the crusades have been fought and continue to be even today. Muslims contend that Ishmael was the proper son and heir as vehemently as Christians believe in the Biblical account naming Isaac, Abraham and Sarah's son of promise.

It is an amazing story of faith and obedience. Please don't be offended if I rehearse the main points again. I don't take for granted that everyone knows the scripture. We are living in a day of great Biblical illiteracy and I am honored to do my part to eradicate that.

Abraham had qualified for AARP twice over. Sarah was right behind him at about ninety years old. They were childless. God promised that the couple would be the first of many generations of special people in God's sight, the Israelites. This was tough with no kids. Abraham and Sarah believed it, sort of. Sarah gave Abraham a girlfriend, believing herself to be well past childbearing years. Along comes Ishmael. God, however, did come through in time, and the miracle child, Isaac, was born to this most unlikely couple.

You have to stop here and appreciate the joy. I love my own children so much it hurts. *Imagine that the idea of having your own child is well beyond hopeless…and then, there he is in your arms looking back up at you.* Come on. Live in the text with me. Smell the baby smell. Take a nap on the couch with the miracle on your stomach. Look into his eyes and see in them the possibility of a tremendous legacy, as many great grandchildren as there are stars in the sky.

Can you imagine the conversations between this "Prince with God" and his friend? "I'm sorry I doubted you, Yahweh. You have made me whole at last." Forget the whole Middle-eastern macho, heir, carry on the bloodline thing. It goes way beyond culture to absolutely revel in the sheer ecstasy of having your own child, healthy with all the fingers and toes…AND HE LOOKS JUST LIKE…*Winston Churchill…oh, well.*

I won't take the time to recount what is very familiar to many of us. If you are foggy on the facts, simply read Genesis, chapters 16 through 22. You can spend a week there, and you should. It is the heart and soul of God's heart and soul.

The story of a man whose commitment and faith were so great that everything was seed, even the baby.

Some time later God tested Abraham. He said to him, "Abraham!"
"Here I am," he replied.
Then God said, "Take your son, your only son, Isaac, whom you love, and go to the region of Moriah. Sacrifice him there as a burnt offering on one of the mountains I will tell you about." Early the next morning Abraham got up and saddled his donkey. He took with him two of his servants and his son Isaac. When he had cut enough wood for the burnt offering, he set out for the place God had told him about. On the third day Abraham looked up and saw the place in the distance. He said to his servants, "Stay here with the donkey while I and the boy go over there. We will worship and then we will come back to you." (Genesis 22:1-5)

How could you even consider it, Abraham? The reality of hindsight takes the punch out of this story. None of us can imagine laying a son on an altar and taking his life with a knife. Those who could most closely identify with it are those who have lost a child to death. How can the rest of us measure the depth of Abraham's faith? What have any of us sacrificed that comes close to the sacrifice this elderly father was prepared to make? What HAS He asked of you that, so far, you have been reluctant to give?

Years ago, I preached a message entitled, "Don't Go There." This phrase had worked its way into our conversation much like, "Get a life" or "Outside the box." I didn't have a particular "there" in mind. It just seems that all of us have something yet unyielded: territory closely guarded, promises not yet kept. We have said our "Lord, send me's" and still haven't gone. There is at least a handful of seed that we clutch in our hand. For most of us, it is not a deep dark secret. No bodies buried in the backyard or secret lives that threaten to be revealed. More likely, there is some good thing, our baby. The truth implied by my old sermon was that "there," whatever or wherever it was, was exactly where we needed to go...maybe for the last time.

Jesus nails it for us in an encounter with an eager young man.

As Jesus started on his way, a man ran up to him and fell on his knees before him. "Good teacher," he asked, "what must I do to inherit eternal life?"

"Why do you call me good?" Jesus answered. "No one is good—except God alone. You know the commandments: 'Do not murder, do not commit adultery, do not steal, do not give false testimony, do not defraud, honor your father and mother."

"Teacher," he declared, "all these I have kept since I was a boy." Jesus looked at him and

loved him. "One thing you lack," he said. "Go, sell everything you have and give to the poor, and you will have treasure in heaven. Then come, follow me." At this the man's face fell. He went away sad, because he had great wealth. (Mark 10:17-22) (emphasis mine)

Don't go there, Jesus. Not that. Not the safety net. You can't have the golden parachute. I worked hard for that. Am I not supposed to be blessed? I prayed to be successful and you and your Father seem to have answered.

Here's the deal. Who knows what would have happened if he HAD been willing. Might Jesus have stopped him? What if he had passed the test like Abraham? We will never know. We do know that Jesus knew, *and the man knew*, and we all know that there was at least one thing the man felt like he couldn't live without, which, being interpreted, means Jesus was an "add on." Another layer. Part and parcel. Abraham, on the other hand, knew that flesh and blood, even that of his promised baby, could not fill that God-shaped gap in his life.

Now the cross is the most compelling example of the faith and commitment it takes to give up the "seed baby." Just consider a short list of what Jesus forfeited at Calvary:

- He gave up the right to be right.
- He relinquished the need for vindication.

- He didn't insist on the last word.
- He denied Himself rescue.
- He allowed people of lesser character to retain the upper hand.
- He resisted any claims to power.
- He refused to humiliate His enemies.
- He suppressed His own will.
- He refused to numb His physical pain.
- He would not lash out at false accusers.
- He released His claim on Divinity.
- The King of Kings allowed Himself to be executed as a common criminal.
- He ignored His own suffering and encouraged the legitimate criminal next to Him.

I am almost ashamed to try to represent some kind of grasp of His sacrifice. I hold so tightly to the seed sometimes. There is great value, though, in trying to wrap our minds around it if only to emphasize how petty we are about what we withhold from Him. We have to somehow try and reconcile this unbelievable level of giving in order to process the possibility of at least a measure of it in our own experience.

Fortunately, the writer to the Hebrews gives us a solution. Jesus did what He did, and Abraham was willing to extinguish the life of the very thing that represented the hope of the promised miracle *BECAUSE THEY UNDERSTOOD THAT WHAT SEED PRODUCED, IF PLANTED, WOULD BE FAR MORE VALUABLE THAN WHAT THE*

SEED PRODUCED IF PROTECTED.

Let us fix our eyes on Jesus, the author and perfecter of our faith, who for the joy set before him endured the cross, scorning its shame, and sat down at the right hand of the throne of God. Consider him who endured such opposition from sinful men, so that you will not grow weary and lose heart. (Hebrews 12:2-3)

Abraham looked into the eyes of the very thing that was too good to be true and His faith compelled him to trust God with it. As painful as giving up his son would be, and although he could not conceive of what would be so precious that it would eclipse the loss of his baby, he let go of the seed.

Jesus looked down through the centuries and saw you…you who are reading these lines and decided that you were worth it. So he drug the cross up the hill, weakened by the loss of blood and lack of nutrition. Naked and alone under the stares and taunting and laughter of godless, hateful, wicked people, the worthy one gave up His life for those who could never be worthy of Him.

Whether or not we surrender the seed, much less allow ourselves to *become* seed, is a declaration of what we really believe. It is not required that we be able to foresee how much more or how much better the harvest will yield if we plant the seed. What He is able and willing to do for us will always remain "immeasurably more than all we ask or imagine…to him be glory in the church and in Christ Jesus throughout all generations, for ever and ever! Amen." *(Ephesians 3:20-21)*

seed biscuit

I sent the following text as an email to our church community during our first series on seed.

You're reading this at your computer at home. If not, you are reading it at work, which means you have a job. Either way, you are doing alright. Not rich, but not poor either. How on earth can we possibly relate to the faith of Abraham or Noah? Sitting in the comfort of our homes or offices is light years away from the agony of the cross. Words like *sacrifice* and *suffering* have no real meaning to us. We have used these terms to describe less and less severe conditions as our lifestyles improve. They cannot come close to approximating anything in our circumstances.

We need for God to blow it up for us. We need a truly spiritual revelation of supernatural proportions to somehow appreciate the depth of what it means to be seed. Drawing from my own experience will never equal the power and the pathos of my Biblical models.

I wash the dishes on occasion. A rare occasion. Maybe once a fortnight, however often that is. You'd think I swam the English Channel towing a barge of orphans to safety. I mean run up the flag. The truth is, I do it just often enough to negate the claim that I "never" help with the housework. But as monumental as that is, can I claim to have loved my wife as "Christ loved the church?" We…I…really am clueless and a long way indeed from being seed.

There is good news, however. I am headed that way and *DIRECTION is more important than DISTANCE.* I will get there, and so will you. Consider the story which inspired this chapter. It is found in 1 Kings.

Then the word of the LORD came to him (Elijah): "Go at once to Zarephath of Sidon and stay there. I have commanded a widow in that place to supply you with food." So he went to Zarephath. When he came to the town gate, a widow was there gathering sticks. He called to her and asked, "Would you bring me a little water in a jar so I may have a drink?"
As she was going to get it, he called, "And bring me, please, a piece of bread."
"As surely as the LORD your God lives," she replied, "I don't have any bread—only a handful of flour in a jar and a little oil in a jug. I am gathering a few sticks to take home and make a meal for myself and my son, that we may eat it—and die."
Elijah said to her, "Don't be afraid. Go home and do as you have said. But first make a small cake of bread for me from what you have and bring it to me, and then make something for yourself

and your son. For this is what the LORD, the God of Israel, says: 'The jar of flour will not be used up and the jug of oil will not run dry until the day the LORD gives rain on the land.'"

She went away and did as Elijah had told her. So there was food every day for Elijah and for the woman and her family. For the jar of flour was not used up and the jug of oil did not run dry, in keeping with the word of the LORD spoken by Elijah. (1 Kings 17:2-16)

"Zarepheth" means *crucible. Crucible* means *a severe test.* If I lived in "Crucible," I'd move. There's nothing in this town a U-Haul wouldn't fix. I'm moving to Prosperity, or *Vegas baby*, or some place. It is in this town that we find two characters, the fiery prophet and the destitute single mom. The prophet is on the move, hungry and thirsty. He should be. He has just walked one hundred miles since his last drink of water.

"Go Elijah," God said. Elijah went. And as we will see, so it goes with the miraculous. I have said it so many times. "Great miracles are often just the other side of a simple act of obedience." Without hesitation, Elijah had LEFT a place of supernatural provision--Cherith (another fascinating story for another set of devotions). *If you are going to make it to second base, you have to let go of first.* "Go to Zarepheth." Elijah hit the trail.

The other hero in this story is our mom with no

means. We are introduced to her gathering firewood…

When he came to the town gate, a widow was there gathering sticks. He called to her and asked, "Would you bring me a little water in a jar so I may have a drink?" As she was going to get it, he called, "And bring me, please, a piece of bread." (1 Kings 17:10-11)

I don't know about you. I've had enough of evangelists wringing the last dollars out of little old ladies. If it had been me, I would have taken my bundle of sticks and beat him to death with it. Not this mom...even though she and her son were one biscuit away from beginning a slow and painful death.

Can we blame her for hesitating?

"As surely as the LORD your God lives," she replied, "I don't have any bread—only a handful of flour in a jar and a little oil in a jug. I am gathering a few sticks to take home and make a meal for myself and my son, that we may eat it—and die." (verse 12)

Two people. Two perspectives. *Are you locked into YOUR way of seeing things?* She saw the impossibilities. Elijah saw what was possible. God had come through at Cherith. He then left for strange and new territory, trusting God. He walked the walk and could therefore talk the talk…

"Don't be afraid. Go home and do as you have said. But first make a small cake of bread for me from what you have and bring it to me, and then make something for yourself and your son.
For this is what the LORD, the God of Israel, says: 'The jar of flour will not be used up and the jug of oil will not run dry until the day the LORD gives rain on the land.' " *(verses 13-14)*

And here is what separates wonder working women from wimpy wannabe's:

She went away and did as Elijah had told her. So there was food every day for Elijah and for the woman and her family. For the jar of flour was not used up and the jug of oil did not run dry, in keeping with the word of the LORD spoken by Elijah. *(verses 15-16)*

Again, she WENT…and she DID.

I have searched the lexicons and thesauruses and delved into dictionaries to find an expression that appropriately expresses my feelings at this moment and I have come up with…cool! That is just cool.

Nothing indicates that the widow and her son opened a phenomenally successful bakery, or that they did anything else but get by on meager means. But we are missing the point, aren't we?

She gave up the last biscuit. She didn't eat the SEED. And in the middle of a drought, she kept three people alive with the residuals from her obedience.

Go ahead. Give him the biscuit. There is more where that came from.

Gethsemane
Ella Wheeler Wilcox

Down shadowy lanes, across strange streams
Bridged over by our broken dreams;
Behind the misty cap of years,
Beyond the great salt fount of tears,
The garden lies. Strive as you may,
You cannot miss it on your way.
All paths that have been, or shall be,
Pass somewhere through Gethsemane.

All those who journey, soon or late,
Must pass within the garden's gate;
Must kneel alone in darkness there,
And battle with some fierce despair.
God pity those who cannot say,
"Not mine but thine," who only pray,
"Let this cup pass," and cannot see
The PURPOSE is Gethsemane.

the bloomin' seed

I have spent a lot of time hanging around with athletic coaches. They tend toward more picturesque speech. Many times, when at a loss to explain how the clumsiest kid made a great catch, or the most awkward youngster exhibited sudden and amazing grace, they would say something to this effect: "Even a blind squirrel can find a nut every now and then." I have always found the expression humorous. I've seen a few of the rodents in my yard and they seem to be quite random in their burial sites for nuts. No rhyme or reason. It follows that, given enough time and enough nuts scattered pall mall throughout the yard, they are bound to get lucky on occasion. I learned the other night that this analogy doesn't fit.

Channel surfing landed me on a human interest documentary. It was a compilation of amazing tragedy to triumph transformations. The third story dealt with a lady who was autistic. Unfortunately, she grew up in the '60s like me and the condition was not understood. It produced a frustrated, misunderstood, socially challenged genius. In spite of her difficult childhood, she has become the nation's foremost authority on the treatment of cattle in stockyards. By trying to understand what a cow sees and experiences, she has literally re-defined the way the industry deals with animals in transport and in the holding pens. What she has discovered has left the cows less stressed--I'm serious--on the way to the slaughter house. This has had a very great effect on the business.

But back to squirrels...Through observation, this amazing lady found that squirrels are not blind, dumb, or lucky. Every time a squirrel buries its prize, it raises up on its haunches and looks around. Apparently, the animal is able to make a mental snapshot of the landmarks in the area. To find a nut, it simply looks around at the scenery until it comes to the same point of view it had when it buried the nut. IT KNOWS WHERE THE SEED IS BURIED.

It occurred to me during a recent quiet time that the difference between stress and calm, depression and joy, is very often a matter of perspective (your point of view). Our circumstances may or may not change, just the way we look at them. I truly believe that much of the satisfaction and fulfillment I feel these days is because I know where I've planted the seed.

My friend, Terry Raburn, told a story in our church several years ago. In Southern Missouri, a soybean farmer invited Terry out to see his spread. They trudged across rows and rows of rich, dark, recently plowed soil. As far as you can see in every direction...dirt. That's all, just dirt. At one point, they stopped. Nothing was said. After an awkward silence, Brother Raburn turned and looked at the guy, who was crying. Huge tears were running down his cheeks and plopping on the ground. For a moment, Terry thought the guy had left his marbles back on the tractor somewhere. After a moment the guy acknowledged, "I guess you think I'm crazy, but I'm not. I just can't help but look at these fields and think about all the seed out there just under the surface."

You could preach it from here. And when the harvest comes, it won't be about luck. He knew where the seed was planted.

For the revelation awaits an appointed time; it speaks of the end and will not prove false. Though it linger, wait for it; it will certainly come and will not delay. (Habakkuk 2:3)

My soul is in anguish.
How long, O LORD, how long? (Psalm 6:3)

Gestation. The period between conception and birth, a dream and its fulfillment, between seed and harvest. This is what makes letting go of the seed so hard. When will the payoff come? How long, O Lord, indeed?

There is no standard answer. While watching the NBC Nightly News a few years ago, I was intrigued by the final story. We saw the desert blooming. Death Valley had suddenly sprung flowers. Hundreds of varieties and brilliant colors were attracting tourists from around the country. People began bringing small children that the reporter told us may have children of their own before the desert sprouts again. It all came together at the right time: rain and sunshine, temperature and soil. "And it will all be gone in a few weeks," the reporter lamented, as the summer sun would soon boil the last of the moisture out of the sand. There was a mention of "hundred year blooms." How long, O Lord?

Sometimes, the return is almost immediate. So many blessings in my life that have come at the peak of my life. I shared that with a friend one day who voiced the fear that some may never see their seed come up. I told him how fortunate I felt to have all that I have and to have experienced so many wonderful moments. "You might believe in luck, or chance, or serendipity," I said, "but I believe that sowing seed brings a harvest, sooner or later."

There seems to be a line that we cross which signals the end of gestation and the beginning of harvest. For many years, I have talked about this threshold. Apparently, some never cross it. This is not as much a point in time as it is an evidence of maturity. It is the point of *unqualified commitment*. It is that place in faith where God knows that we know that He knows we are not going back. We have made our choice. It is HIS seed. We truly place it in HIS hands for a field of HIS choosing.

I asked a young believer if he knew the story of Shadrach, Meshach and Abednego. These guys were scheduled for extermination. In a haunting foreshadow of 20th century holocaust, a huge furnace was kindled to burn them alive. They had crossed the line. *But they got it.* "Our God is able to deliver us!" What a testimony! "He will deliver us!" Now that takes it to another level. They had catapulted up the pyramid to a rarified level. They declared their faith openly. But then, they showed us that they were committed without reservation. "But even if He doesn't, we will not bow down to a pagan king." These guys sowed seed in their first two statements. They proved they WERE WILLING TO <u>BE SEED</u> WITH THEIR FINAL WORDS.

God showed up. He went into the fire with them and walked them out alive.

The day of Pentecost came. Not because they reached a specific day, but because they crossed the line. Jesus made a promise. They weren't leaving until it came. Who knows? They might have stayed there until some day, years later, someone found their bodies or their bones. He said, "Wait."
How long, O Lord?

Not long, now. Not long.

It is a rather narrow understanding of seed to think of it only as money. It is anything that we value really. It could be time or energy, passion or compassion. What is even more significant is the fact that seed is not just something that we give, but that we can be.

Until we are spent, we cannot say we have done all that we can do. To acknowledge that, having exhausted all my resources, I yet have something to contribute is a huge responsibility.

"Pastor Bill, I am writing this to you with tears streaming down my face. Steve Hill, the evangelist associated with The Brownsville Outpouring, speaks many times of the seed you sowed into his life. As a recovering addict, you asked him to play the part of Jesus in your Easter program. When I think of the hundreds of thousands of people who have come to know Christ through Pastor Steve's, ministry I am amazed at the power of a little seed. Daniel and I will always be grateful for the seed you sowed in our lives." --Jenna Norris

cloud seeding

(An email to the church)

It is hard to imagine drought when it is raining and cold. Drought happens though, to all of us. There are long dry spells. Let it rain, Lord, please. I am dry and thirsty, Lord, send your rain.

You could do a rain dance I guess. Build a fire. Shake your fist at the sky. Wash your car. We all know that works. Or, you could seed the clouds.

> **cloud seeding. The American Heritage® Dictionary of the English Language: Fourth Edition. 2000.**
> ...A technique of stimulating or enhancing precipitation by distributing dry ice crystals or silver iodide particles over developing storm clouds in a specific area...

It might rain if you seeded the clouds. Worth a try, isn't it?

Right before church tonight, I told Cindy that I didn't have a clue about what to write for today. What happens if the well dries up and I am at a loss? I don't want to waste your time. I would hate for you to open this mail, only to find it weak and shallow. Every night, I hope that I haven't gotten the last of the oil from the cruse and the meal from the barrel. I have a keen sense of responsibility to write something worth reading. Oh, I have an outline. There are phrases that I have written that are the catalysts for chapters to come. I have said it before, I want *THE* word and not just *A* word. And during the worship tonight, I thought of cloud seeding. It is the first time that phrase has occurred to me and I had to wonder if it was about you.

Clouds. A metaphor for gloom. Clouds sometimes represent a hindrance. Our judgement becomes "clouded." The warming rays of sunshine are sometimes blocked by the clouds. Clouds might mean hope and despair at the same time. In a drought, a cloud brings the hope of rain, yet that rain might not come. The potential is there, just no rain.

There are clouds that have obscured our vision. It is hard to see through them as they hover over our kids. A cloud hangs in the hospital room where the prognosis is not good. Hope fades. Visions die. Dreams go unrealized. A perpetual cloud seems to follow us like Charlie Brown's hapless friend. Still, no rain.

Seed the clouds.

Our seed is praise. In the middle of the gray-light we lift our hands and shout "Grace" anyway. God arrives on the scene. He was waiting to be invited in. He brings with Him rain. Go on. Stare the cloud in the face and declare the Glory of God. Bring your umbrella.

I love to tell the story. We all know it well. Paul
and Silas in prison at midnight. Cloudy in there.
They get a grip and let it rip. They sing. The
earth moves. The prison doors fly open. They
sit there in the rain. My imagination has often
led me to speculate what might have happened.
Through the clouds, the Father hears his praise.
Like a mother who can discern the cry of HER
child above every other child, or a freight train
for that matter, He hears His guys, and He runs
toward them with the rain. His feet cause the
earth to quake. The prisoners are freed.

You know who you are. Are those tears? Yes,
you.

Seed the clouds.
Here comes the rain.
I love you all…Pastor Bill

…and the next day I wrote:

This is Friday! I hope that yours is great. I am
so grateful to those of you who respond with a
word of encouragement to me. Every night, I sit
here and prayerfully key in the word I sense God
is giving me. When you reply that I've nailed it,
you can't imagine how much that means to me.
God is faithful. He knows where you are. In a

few moments, I will hit the "send" and then hit the sheets. Fresh inspiration awaits me tomorrow because our Father will be up all night, thinking of ways to show you, each of you, how uniquely He knows and loves you.

I stood on the hill today and observed the deep, gray blanket of cloud covering that reached the horizon all around me. On impulse, I stretched my arm out and up, turning my palm toward my face. Why? I wanted to see how much sky would be obscured by my hand at arm's length from my eyes. It didn't cover much. I'd have to say that my hand was overwhelmed by the expanse of sky by many times. Interesting.

And Elijah said to Ahab, "Go, eat and drink, for there is the sound of a heavy rain." So Ahab went off to eat and drink, but Elijah climbed to the top of Carmel, bent down to the ground and put his face between his knees.
"Go and look toward the sea," he told his servant. And he went up and looked.
"There is nothing there," he said.
Seven times Elijah said, "Go back."
The seventh time the servant reported, "A cloud as small as a man's hand is rising from the sea."
So Elijah said, "Go and tell Ahab, 'Hitch up your chariot and go down before the rain stops you."
Meanwhile, the sky grew black with clouds, the wind rose, a heavy rain came on and Ahab rode off to Jezreel. (1 Kings 18:41-45)

Elijah "prayed through." Or, you might say he prayed until he got through. Seven times *anything* represents that which is full or complete in scripture. We can only speculate what Elijah prayed following that incredible demonstration of fire on Mt. Carmel (read the book). He probably seeded the cloud with some praise. God had just shown up and restored his altar and his honor before the people. He might have prayed for protection as he returned to Jezreel to face Jezebel. One thing is certain, he prayed for rain.

None in the forecast, though. Not a cloud in the sky. "In your name, Amen." Then he sent his associate pastor to look in the sky. "Clear as a bell, your eminence" (showing the proper respect for the senior pastor). So the prophet prayed again...and again. After about five or six times, the associate pastor began having déjà vu all over again. Seems the prophets of Baal had prayed, *and* shouted, *and* danced, *and* cut themselves all day, and nothing happened. Tragically, younger ministers lack the faith that their more experienced mentors have. "One more time," the old seasoned prayer warrior challenged.

Well, what do you know! A cloud. A little one, but a cloud just the same. Elijah had already sent the wimp King Ahab back towards town so that he wouldn't get wet. Too late. The bottom fell out. It was about time. Drought had all but devastated the place. It had come full circle. The prophet had told the king it wouldn't rain until he (Elijah) said it would. That day, God confirmed His Word, *and* His man, *and* His sovereignty.

The prophet got up from the place of prayer, praying until he knew the answer had come. He saw just a little indication of the remote possibility of a little moisture, and then he made his declaration of faith. HE LITERALLY SEEDED THE CLOUD.

And he ran home, in the rain.

It's beginning to rain, church. Let's run.

I have been preaching on Simon, "The Rock." Most Christians are familiar with the excesses of this colorful character. The first in and the first out. He asked a lot of questions and had a lot of answers, whether they were wanted or not. Voted "Most Likely to Goof Up" by those who have not read beyond the Gospels. I am reminded when I look at *The Passion of the Christ,* that much of our culture only knows the Bible basics, the condensed version. We must work against the Biblical illiteracy that is common in our world. There is so much more to Peter's story than his brief experience in the actual company of Jesus.

For years now, I have been looking at the man from both sides of Pentecost. Of all the incidents of spiritual or emotional upheaval that seem to punctuate his instability, nothing seems to define the former fisherman more than this monumental manifestation of the Holy Spirit. I won't take the time here to do "before and after" comparisons. All you have to do is read his two letters, 1 Peter and 2 Peter. The evidence of the value of that experience is amazing and conclusive.

There is one highlight from his life that I would like to visit again, perhaps because it is the one I relate to the most. Peter was **so confident** that he would not fold under pressure like the rest of the group. My dad used to say to me, "Lesser men couldn't have done it" after we hiked the mountain or conquered the yard work. My dad didn't really take himself that seriously. Peter, on the other hand, **believed** that all the other men were lesser men. WHAT A BLOW TO DISCOVER THAT YOU ARE AN ORDINARY PERSON, not fearless, invincible or perfect. HOW COULD HE DEAL WITH THE FACT THAT JESUS' GREATEST DISAPPOINTMENT HAD TURNED OUT TO BE "THE ROCK?"

Mel Gibson's epic reminds us, though it is subtle, that eye contact was made. Jesus and the arrogant fisherman locked eyes and Peter came face to face with his failure to produce. The man who obviously felt he could handle any situation, any threat, who took out his sword and severed Malchus' ear, now wilted at the taunts of a milk maid. He couldn't help Jesus. He had to save his own skin…take care of #1, just like the most cowardly and common of men. He didn't measure up after all. He wasn't made of the right stuff.

So Peter reverted to something simpler. It could be that he just needed to master something that he had succeeded at before. Break a sweat. Mend a net. Load up the boat and we are back in business. I guess it's over after all. Yes, go back to the boat and recover a little of your dignity. Back to the lake and being king of the village. IF YOU MAKE NO CLAIMS TO BEING A SPIRITUAL LEADER, THERE WILL BE NO CLAIMS TO BACK UP.

Been there. Done that. Bought the T-shirt. Sold it at a yard sale. Somebody re-gifted it and gave it to me for Christmas. I dropped the ball. I didn't meet my own expectations, much less the one who died for me that day.

It is called "love hunger" and everyone who has medicated their pain with food, alcohol, shopping, working, or taking risks will connect with Peter right here. Deflect it, deny it, drown it out if you can; it just isn't going away. In reality, no amount of fish can compensate for the pain I feel KNOWING I let Him down. I cannot recuperate and will never recover.

There is ONE thing…one hope…one possibility. If HE gave me another shot. If I could hear it directly from Him. If I could look in His face…

"I'd lay it all down, again. Just to hear Him say that 'I'm your friend'"…

Now my sons are serious athletes. Stars in high school, college, and my son Bo appeared as a football hero in the movie *Radio*. My daughter Hannah, bless her heart, inherited her dad's athletic ability. I used to kid her about "walking track" in high school. Concerning my athletic career, the scouting report on me was that I was "quite short, yet slow." As a matter of fact, I quit football because I wasn't good enough to play. I got frustrated with being a tackling dummy at practice. My mom never had to wash my game pants unless I stumbled getting off the bus. I haven't quit anything since then. The week after I quit football, our team got so far ahead by the half that the coach played everyone except the cheerleaders. I made up my mind that I would never, ever quit again.

Peter quit. That's why I love this story so much. "I'm going fishing, guys. I'm not cut out for this." He went for the comfort food. Reached for the cookies and ice cream. At least a boat-load of fish would serve as tangible evidence that he'd been there and served some purpose. Things haven't changed much in 2,000 years. It didn't work for Peter, and it doesn't work for me. It doesn't work for any of you either and, in this reality, I find part of my life's mission.

It's human nature. That is Christian-speak for "I can't seem to help myself." It is the Christian's excuse. We don't dare finish the race last, so we pull up lame. We don't want to deal with the fact that we haven't followed through, so we quit, offering any number of "human nature" explanations. Here are the ones I have heard most:

- I don't have the time to do it justice (*So don't even try???*)

- I need to let someone younger, better, or more talented do it.
- I need to spend more time with my family.
- I'm not cut out for this. This is not really my ministry, or calling.
- I've really dropped the ball…in over my head… didn't know what I was committing to.

That "human nature" is strong stuff. It got the best of me in football. It won't again.

Peter had pulled up lame. He had resigned his position. He quit. But the story doesn't end there. Jesus didn't let him quit. I love that. I'm a long way from being like Jesus, but I do relate to that. Much of my counsel over the years has been given in an effort to discourage quitting. JUST TODAY, I was able to challenge a brother who felt badly about running a poor race. I felt compelled to tell him to GRADUATE RATHER THAN GIVE UP. If it has whipped you so far, fight off that horrible "human" nature and MASTER IT.

Some have criticized me for it. Some think I tolerate more than I should. There are those who would like to see me crack the whip, lay down the law and get rid of the dead weight. BUT I HAVE REALIZED THAT GOD CAN MAKE DEAD WEIGHT LIVE. I am guilty of hoping that people would not accept failure. I am driven by the need to give the time and the grace and the encouragement so men, especially men, would shake off past mistakes, renew the race and finish. No regrets.

When Peter needed tax money, he learned that Jesus was the SOURCE. When Peter felt like fishing might ease the pain of his failure, he failed at that too. John 21 says he caught NOTHING...nada, zilch, zero. What do you do when there is no comfort in the comfort food? Jesus comes. Need fish? Got some on the fire. What do YOU think is harder, fried fish for breakfast or a fish with the temple tax in its mouth? Jesus comforts, but He doesn't let you quit.

John tells us that Jesus yelled from the shore. He wanted them to try the "right" side of the boat. They did. They filled the nets. Déjà vu! John remembered and shouted his recognition. Jesus had done the same thing when he called them to be "fishers of men," eighteen months earlier. And PETER...did something HE had done before. He jumped out of the boat to get to Jesus. John's gospel tells us that he swam, fully clothed, the remaining one hundred yards to the beach.

In a moment, the first personal words between Simon Peter and his resurrected Savior were exchanged. But first...

*Jesus said to them, 'Come and have breakfast.'"
None of the disciples dared ask him, "Who are
you?" They knew it was the Lord. Jesus came,
took the bread and gave it to them, and did the
same with the fish.* (John 21:12-13)

Please allow me to amplify the text. I just can't
help but see myself in Peter's wet sandals.
Could it be that he would have another chance,
a fresh start? Put me in coach, I'm READY to
play. I won't drop the ball this time. And he
wouldn't.

The poignant exchange in John 21 includes
three declarations of love for Jesus, one for
each denial. We have come full circle. The
sifting has occurred. Peter...has become seed.
*And remember the regenerative power in the
seed. Everything needed for the seed to make
more seed is IN THE SEED.*

Everything you think might fill the void or ease
the pain is with Jesus. Feed the sheep. Be the
seed.

God assigns inestimable value to those who
realize their value as seed.

Seed you later.

the seed fish

You can't imagine how I have resisted going to this illustration. I was telling Pastor Chris this morning over coffee that it seemed so obvious that I could have any one of our Kid's Church children draw the parallels with sowing seed and the little boy's lunch. The truth is, and I didn't realize it until this morning, that my pride was getting in the way of a fresh look at this familiar story.

I've preached it from almost every angle. From the disciples' lack of faith to the little boy's sincere offering, I've turned it inside out. I've even found some humor in it. I used to joke that I could perform an updated version of the miracle by feeding 5,000 teens with a few anchovy pizzas. Anchovies are the key. One bite and you'll take a pass on the next one. In 1980, I wrote a drama in which I speculated about the boy growing up, his poor family sustained by the business which started from the leftover baskets. An old man now, the play is built on his memory of the event, complete with souvenir crusts of bread and fish bones in a pouch around his neck. I haven't thought of that in years. Somebody's email will let me know why it has come to the surface today.

For those of you who are just discovering the wonders of the Bible, here is the text:

As evening approached, the disciples came to him and said, "This is a remote place, and it's already getting late. Send the crowds away, so they can go to the villages and buy themselves some food."
Jesus replied, "They do not need to go away. You give them something to eat."
"We have here only five loaves of bread and two fish," they answered.
"Bring them here to me," he said. And he directed the people to sit down on the grass. Taking the five loaves and the two fish and looking up to heaven, he gave thanks and broke the loaves. Then he gave them to the disciples, and the disciples gave them to the people. They all ate and were satisfied, and the disciples picked up twelve basketfuls of broken pieces that were left over. The number of those who ate was about five thousand men, besides women and children. (Matthew 14:15-21)

There are some powerful symbols here. In the desert, God miraculously provided Manna (bread) for the Israelites (Exodus 16). Elisha fed one hundred men in a supernatural event. Manna is clearly associated with the Messiah. That is true for both Jews and Christians. There is no doubt that this is a deliberate declaration of Jesus' Messianic status. Every Sunday, we celebrate Communion, recalling a meal in which Jesus also "took bread, gave thanks, and broke it."

There is so much here. He actually did it twice. The second mass feeding miracle was for 4,000 men and their families. The second time, however, the crowd who received the bread was Gentile, as opposed to the 5,000 Jewish men on the initial occasion. Whosoever will may come. Hallelujah.

Even as a child, I wondered how it worked. Did it multiply in the basket, out of sight of the crowd? Did it grow in front of their eyes? Was everyone distracted as Jesus continued to tear portions from the same loaf?

All I know for sure is that it somehow happened *as it passed through His hands.* In the boy's lunch pail, it was and forever would be five loaves and two small fish. When it *left the boys hands and was committed into the hands of Jesus,* it somehow fed as many as 15,000 people.

Once more, the Lord is placing an explanation point on one of the truths dearest to HIM. Let go of the seed. The old song says, "Little is much when God is in it." ISN'T THERE MUCH MORE JOY IN FEEDING A MULTITUDE THAN YOU CAN EXPERIENCE BY CONSUMING YOUR LUNCH?

Ten percent of your income will always be ten percent until you give it back to Him. It starts with Him...everything belongs to the Lord. It is ten percent when He conveys it into our hands. What is so little in the face of such great need? Let it go and you will find out. Harvest trumps lunch all day long.

Terri Schiavo.

Try and find someone who doesn't know that name. Her plight dominated the news.

This is what I wrote at the time.

CNN is constantly updating the audience on the state of the appeals to reinsert her feeding tube. It is on all four TV's at Gold's Gym. I went home and it is the subject of conversation in my den. It's on the front page of the paper. It has been discussed, I'm sure, in your work place. Do you think you know what I am going to say about this? I'm probably going to surprise you.

Mary Reames and Lindsey, my daughters-in-law, made a couple of very cogent points. The first being that we don't know enough. What we know is shown out of context. Another good point is that you really have to experience the drama in real life before you can understand what it is all about. You don't really know until you've been there with someone you love, and I have, as have some of you.

No, I'm not going to take a position on the morals

here. What I want to leave with you today is how profoundly ONE PERSON can impact the culture. The closest example of this is, of course, Terri Schiavo. Friday is Day Eight. Any moment now, someone could make the decision that allows her to live. In the meantime, she lies suspended between two passionate, even bitter arguments. Each side claims to have the moral high ground. Sound familiar? In *The Passion of the Christ,* Pilate asks Jesus and then his troubled wife, "What is truth?"

Pilate sought the middle ground. There is no such thing. Neither he nor Herod, Israel's puppet king were willing to take a stand and save his life *NOR* condemn Him to die. As I write, Terri Schiavo's case is bouncing from civil court to Supreme Court. Even the congress was not willing to put enough bite in their resolution to force the issue. However, there is no shortage of "holy" people who plead "God's interest" and claim His perspective on the dilemma. I want you to know that they may or may not speak for me.

Once again, the nation is divided, as fickle in their faith as the citizens of Jerusalem were that last week of Jesus' life. Within the space of five days, the same crowd went from "Hosanna" (save us) to "Kill Him." We could go on and on drawing parallels here.

But I must emphasize how incredibly different

these two stories are. Yes, a single person, like a single seed can make a huge impact. BUT, REGARDLESS OF WHETHER OR NOT TERRI SCHIAVO DIES, IT WILL BE FORGOTTEN IN A FEW MONTHS. Whether the "Right to Lifers" have their way or the "Die with Dignity" crowd claim a victory here, it will make very little difference.

Jesus' life and death, on the other hand, made ALL the difference. The thirty-three years from his birth to his death and resurrection DIVIDE ALL OF HISTORY into before and after. Ten years from now, we won't refer to Schiavo as a watershed moment in history. We will STILL, however, be offering our lives as seed in His Kingdom. We will still weep at the thought of His suffering and cruel death. We will still shout at the 1972 years old pronouncement that "He is not here. He is risen."

Once again, forgive me for borrowing the words of a poem, made into a song in the '70s. I started to just share the last few phrases, but...

He was born in an obscure village, the child of a peasant woman. He grew up in another obscure village, where He worked in a carpenter shop until he was 30. Then for three years He was an itinerant preacher. He never had any family or owned a home. He never set foot inside a big city. He never traveled two hundred miles from the place He was born. He never wrote a book, or held an office.

He did none of the things that usually accompany greatness.

When He was still a young man, the tide of popular opinion turned against Him. His friends deserted Him. He was turned over to His enemies, and went through the mockery of a trial. He was nailed to a cross between two thieves. While He was dying, His executioners gambled for the only piece of property He had--His coat. When He was dead, He was taken down and laid in a borrowed grave.

Nineteen centuries have come and gone, and today He is still the central figure of much of the human race. All the armies that ever marched and all the navies that ever sailed and all the parliaments that ever sat and all the kings that ever reigned, put together, have not affected the life of mankind upon this earth as powerfully as this "ONE SOLITARY LIFE." -- *James A. Francis*

We begin Day 26…

How many times have you said it? "Things didn't turn out like I'd planned." It is possible that we deceive ourselves. In reality, things turn out exactly in accordance with our plans. What we are really saying sometimes is that we haven't planned at all. We shouldn't be surprised if a previous lack of purpose has left us floundering with excess emotional, physical, or even financial baggage.

As we were preparing for Vision Sunday a couple of years ago, Pastor Chris reviewed video of the previous year's projections. He commented that it seemed almost as if I were a prophet and could see the future. In a way, I can, and so can you. We shouldn't be amazed when we plant corn and harvest corn. You plant okra, you get okra. As you have heard all of your life, "You reap WHAT you sow." It is harvest law.

Another immutable law is that you harvest MORE than you plant. A kernel of corn produces a stalk. A single offering produces 30, 60, or 100 fold. One solitary life invested in His name can yield a harvest. That is the up side. It is that hope that keeps us sowing into the Kingdom. Give and it will be given back to you... "good measure" (think of a bushel basket), "pressed down," (pushed and compacted, making room for more), "shaken together" (so that settling occurs, using every space, making room for more), and "running over." You're going to need bigger baskets and bigger barns.

All of this is great news, if you are sowing good seed. The law applies though, to the bad seed as well. This is born out in Hosea's prophecy concerning Israel. Listen to his dark prediction:

"They sow the wind...and reap the whirlwind."
(Hosea 8:7)

Hosea is a master of the comparative analogy. It is another way of emphasizing the first law of harvest: reaping more than you sow. The Hebrew lexicon says the word for *wind* here could mean "breath" and *whirlwind*, a "hurricane." So it is with bad seed and good. Depending on the seed you sow, there could be a "blessing you cannot contain" or a harvest of trouble. More often than not, the future is mortgaged for a momentary pleasure. No wonder some say that you sow wild oats and then pray for crop failure.

This is a harvest of heartbreak. I see it everyday. It is enough, sometimes, to discourage and derail good people. They thought everything would change when they became a believer. They thought the shadows and skeletons would all disappear. They don't. We shouldn't be surprised.

I was reminded of this today in two ways. The first, by a broken heart, with questions and pain and disenchantment. I will help if I can. The second, was graphically represented in the final moment of *The Passion of the Christ.* As Jesus rises from his place in the tomb, we see the scars from the nails through His hands. As you know, He would later invite His disciples to inspect the nail imprints as He appeared to them after the resurrection. The point is not lost on me. Sometimes the scars remain, if not the bitter fallout from bad decisions and poor choices.

Don't blame God. Don't blame anyone. Just sow better seed. We will plow through this harvest of tears somehow. We will do it together. All the while we will frustrate our enemy who would love us to be his trophy. It won't happen. A harvest of righteousness is on its way.

leproseed

You were created to pursue grand and noble things. *No one is called to mediocrity and there is no anointing for doing nothing--only death.*

Now there were four men with leprosy at the entrance of the city gate. They said to each other, "Why stay here until we die? If we say, 'We'll go into the city'—the famine is there, and we will die. And if we stay here, we will die. So let's go over to the camp of the Arameans and surrender. If they spare us, we live; if they kill us, then we die."

At dusk they got up and went to the camp of the Arameans. When they reached the edge of the camp, not a man was there, for the Lord had caused the Arameans to hear the sound of chariots and horses and a great army, so that they said to one another, "Look, the king of Israel has hired the Hittite and Egyptian kings to attack us!"

So they got up and fled in the dusk and abandoned their tents and their horses and donkeys. They left the camp as it was and ran for their lives.

The men who had leprosy reached the edge of the camp and entered one of the tents. They ate and drank, and carried away silver,

gold and clothes, and went off and hid them.
They returned and entered another tent and
took some things from it and hid them also.
Then they said to each other, "We're not doing
right. This is a day of good news and we are
keeping it to ourselves. If we wait until daylight,
punishment will overtake us. Let's go at once
and report this to the royal palace."
(2 Kings 7:3-9)

War is hell. Siege warfare is the most horrific and
cruel strategy that a bloodthirsty culture could
possibly prosecute. It is a war of attrition. It is
truly an unstoppable force versus an immovable
object. The invaders cannot breach the city
defenses. So they just camp outside, no one in
or out, until the people inside starve to death.

The old and infirm die first, followed quickly by
the infants and toddlers. Distended bellies and
sunken eyes. You'd think that there would be
a measure of compassion. Let the women and
children go. But no. War is hell. The horror is
evident in the previous chapter:

As the king of Israel was passing by on the
wall, a woman cried to him, "Help me, my lord
the king!"... Then he asked her, "What's the
matter?" She answered, "This woman said to
me, 'Give up your son so we may eat him today,
and tomorrow we'll eat my son.' So we cooked
my son and ate him. The next day I said to her,
'Give up your son so we may eat him,' but she

had hidden him. *(2 Kings 6:26-29)*

This sets the dark scene as a quartet of hopeless lepers discuss their plight. They are caught in the crossfire. They had no place to go. Siege or no siege they had no refuge among their own people because of their leprosy. Their fate seemed to be a slow death in no man's land outside the gate.

Then something extraordinary happened. The conversation produced a plan born of desperation. It wasn't about nobility or courage. Death was certain. The "born to lose" had nothing to lose by seeking a measure of control over their own destiny. Ultimately, one said to the other three, "Let's roll."

It took a while for reality to set in. They survived the hike and were now standing in the enemy's camp. No one was guarding the stuff. There was food on the stove and treasure in the tents. They took a walk and ended up millionaires. They owned the place and its plunder. There was no way that they could have envisioned this. Even if they had, they lacked the resources to get it done. We have a 20/20 perspective on the narrative, but there is no way they could explain what had just happened to them. They couldn't have produced this result if they tried for a lifetime.

This reminds me of a rather amazing grace.

I have a story to tell about liberation and prosperity. There was not anything I could have done to acquire my freedom. I cannot really explain how I came to the place of the incredible blessing that I am walking in now. I just shake my head weeping and rejoicing at the wonder of it all. I once was lost. Not any more.

Can you remember the instant when you realized you were truly free? There has to be a moment when the light comes on and we get it. I'm not just talking about our liberation, but about the obligation we have to those who are still under siege in the city. Do you *get that yet?* We owe! What we've found must be shared--and quickly. It is a matter of life and death. The desperate lepers in the Biblical account realized that their neighbors were still prisoners in their own city. The desperate status had not changed. Only now, they were held captive by their fear and their lack of knowledge. *What they didn't know was killing them.* These men knew the truth that would set the city free.

Please note a couple of things that these guys wrestled with before doing the right thing. We struggle with and must process these two things in our own context. First, it doesn't matter how we were treated when we were lepers, we still have to tell them. And second, it must not matter if we don't receive the credit, we still have to tell them.

It really doesn't get any better than this. FREEDOM! I'm truly free and I get to eat at the King's table--but there is more. I get to tell people that they're free—the lost... the bound, the blind, the frightened, the broken, the bewildered, the discouraged, the depressed, the disenfranchised, the marginalized, the unloved, the unlovely, the wounded, the broken, the beaten, the bloodied, the people next to me in the store, the athletes on the field of play, the neighbors where I live, and the people around the corner and the people around the world. YOU CAN BE FREE! TO THOSE WHO DON'T KNOW WHERE THEY ARE MUCH LESS WHERE THEY ARE GOING, TO THOSE WHO HAVE LOST THE STRENGTH FOR WAKING UP IN THE MORNING, for those who have no motivation to fight for change, no power to endure, THERE IS HOPE. GET UP. GET BACK IN IT. YOU'RE FREE!

Expectations can wear us out and leave us disappointed. Failed expectations between husbands and wives can shipwreck a marriage. We even become slaves to personal expectations regarding income and status which, if not realized, leave us feeling like failures. For all of us who know the disappointment of unrealistic or unfulfilled expectations, I've created a new word. The word is *nextpectation*. The idea I hope to express is a sense of breathless anticipation that God is going to do even more amazing things than we have ever experienced before. *What could be next?* We know it will be great and that it will benefit us far beyond what we could ask for or expect. A sense of *nextpectancy* can be entertained because God has built incredible promise into the seed.

Paul's conversation with the Corinthians on sowing and seed is nothing less than a manifesto from God regarding harvest. I cannot help but be overwhelmed by *nextpectation* as I read the following passage. When I shared it with my church family recently, I asked the congregation to stand because of the majesty of it.

Remember this: Whoever sows sparingly will also reap sparingly, and whoever sows generously will also reap generously.
Each man should give what he has decided in his heart to give, not reluctantly or under compulsion, for God loves a cheerful giver.
(2 Corinthians 9:6-7)

Those two verses need no exposition. They are simple and clear. The next verses, however, provide broad and glorious vistas of the landscape of God's heart and will provide a wealth of information about the *why* behind the life in the seed.

And God is able to make all grace abound to you, so that in all things at all times, having all that you need, you will abound in every good work. *(2 Corinthians 9:8)* (emphasis mine)

What can *"all grace"* mean? I can only say that God is making it happen for me more and more everyday. It is resources and provision, both spiritual and material. It is enough and more than enough. It overlaps and touches every area of my life. I realize that I don't know what it truly means to be seed, but I do know that the grace God abounds toward me is nothing short of amazing. *Grace* has come to be an all-inclusive term which encompasses the many, many blessings of my life. My family. My church family. It is the incredible gift of KNOWING and then the privilege of PURSUING my purpose as well. *It would cheapen the word grace by simply listing financial blessings.* I'm talking about emotional, physical and spiritual surpluses that enable me to participate significantly in GOOD WORK! And on it goes in verse eight, "in ALL things...at ALL times, having ALL you need."

On the back cover of this book you will see a picture of a basket being overrun by falling seed. This has become an icon in our church. I'll never forget a sleepless night trying to think of a way to illustrate "good measure, pressed down, shaken together and running over" *(Luke 6:38).* In my mind, I sketched a plan for a seed bin with a trap door that would allow a lot of seed to fall steadily over several minutes. I wanted to suspend the rig from the ceiling, concealing it until the moment of release. On cue, the seed would begin to fill the basket. The design worked. Now, the moment is forever imprinted on our hearts and minds.

I can close my eyes now and hear the sound of two hundred pounds of seed corn dropping twenty feet, filling, and then overwhelming a bushel basket. The sound was surprisingly loud, a little like rain falling on a sheet metal roof. Some seed bounced into the second and third rows of seats. It fell for seven minutes, burying the basket and cascading down the platform steps. I turned to see the reaction and was amazed to see people weeping--some even standing--as the reality of God's promise broke upon them in a fresh way.

I had a private conversation with my God and asked Him to allow me to be a seed. I didn't have to be a bushel basket. If He would allow me, I would dream the dream, and like David *(2 Samuel 7)*, be content to leave the fulfillment of the dream to my sons. If I can somehow provide the portal through which young ministers pass in order to discover great harvest on the other side, then I will have known the great grace and unbelievable joy that no other pursuit could have realized.

If heaven is a myth, I still want to be seed. If the only joy remaining for me is to see the *potential* of a seedling, and not *potential realized* in the harvest, then I have experienced enough joy to leave any man content. If I can just pass through His hands, on the way to a place of HIS choosing, I at least will know that I have the fingerprints of God on me. What else could I aspire to?

More creative scribes than I have tried to get their minds around the incredible concept of abounding grace.

"O for a thousand tongues to sing, my great Redeemer's praise; the glories of my God and King, the triumphs of His grace."
--Charles Wesley

"Could we with ink the ocean fill, and were the skies of parchment made. Were every stalk on earth a quill and every man a scribe by trade. To write the love of God above would drain the oceans dry." *--Frederick Lehman*

Trying to quantify "all grace" would be like attempting to explain the volume of the ocean in terms of quarts. How could you even begin? Eugene Peterson's translation of this verse reads, *"God can pour blessings in astonishing ways..."* (*2 Corinthians 9:8, The Message*)

"Now <u>He who supplies seed</u> to the sower and <u>bread</u> for food will also supply and increase your store of seed and will enlarge the <u>harvest of your righteousness.</u>" (*2 Corinthians 9:10*)
(emphasis mine)

At the risk of redundancy, I say again, it's *not your seed.* We have to settle the ownership issue or never know the incredible flow of resources that the Father stands ready to initiate through us. We have to release it so that *it and you* may conform to our divine design. We really don't understand it. We do the math and it doesn't work. Why is He willing to send and renew this unbelievably empowering supply? The answer lies in the fact that **He is going to see that the harvest is funded.** If we will sow the seed, He will supply more seed and **bread as well!** To my shame, I have been so self-absorbed and shallow that I was worried there wouldn't be enough bread.

Notice that the goal is the *harvest of your righteousness.* And, in addition to my spiritual maturity, the next verse presents another reason for supplying and renewing our seed.

You will be made rich in every way so that you can be generous on every occasion, and through us your generosity will result in thanksgiving to God. (2 Corinthians 9:11)

Don't miss the *"through us"* qualifier. The seed we sow has been supplied for harvest. The church and its leadership is uniquely equipped to validate needs and targets for our generosity. Once again, as products of our culture, we resist any direction concerning the resources of time, talent or finance that God has entrusted to us. Is it possible that we could nullify His promise of grace by insisting on imposing our will on the disposition of the seed? As a pastor, I have grieved over legitimate needs which go lacking because well-intentioned people have funded pet projects and rejected counsel.

I understand how you might feel that this is a bit self-serving coming from a pastor. Allow me to give you an example that will illustrate why we must sow our seed within the context of a local church and under the guidance of God's leaders.

In 1972, I made my first missions trip. The site was Bogotá, Colombia in a desperately poor "barrio" on the outskirts of the city. Everyday, we encountered horrific scenes of children who appeared to make their homes in the streets. Many of the children had deformed or missing limbs. Our hearts were broken for them and their pitiful condition. On several occasions, I reached in my pocket and gave sufficient dollars to make a real difference in a country whose per capita income was less than fifty dollars per month at that time. It felt good. It brought instant gratification to think that I had been a benefactor and must have appeared *"rich in every way."* That was, however, before I understood why *"through us"* is such a vital component of effective sowing.

I didn't realize that the mean streets of Bogota produced an unthinkable and inhuman business enterprise. The missionary in residence had observed us giving the money to these pitiful kids and gathered us together to explain why we shouldn't have done it. Until humanitarian agencies were able to generate political pressure on the local government in Colombia's major cities in order to shut down the practice, people actually produced children for the purpose of begging and so maimed them at birth. Obviously, the disfiguring evoked more sympathy and produced more money on the street. If I had given enough for a prosthetic limb, the child would never have received it. All I had done, despite my sincerity, was help to perpetuate the sickening exploitation of these precious children. At fifteen, I learned a lesson that has lasted until now. And, as a pastor, I have a unique perspective and, many times, a lot more information that would help guide sincere givers in being good stewards of the seed.

For those who are generous with the seed and will accept guidance concerning appropriate opportunities, the seed never runs out. We initiate the flow by letting go of what He has entrusted to us. He will keep us supplied if we keep it flowing. Our time is redeemed. Our finances are renewed by unexpected and supernatural means. The emotional capital we invest will be returned to us many times over if we will sow the seed into the Kingdom.

Paul assures us that *"...your generosity will result in thanksgiving to God" (2 Corinthians 9:11).* The people who are blessed through your time, energy, or other resources certainly do not live in a vacuum. They will praise God for you, and others will hear. When we meet legitimate needs where accountability is attached to the gift, we can be assured that we have done well. We can know that a ground swell of thanksgiving will be offered up to the Father, a praise that fills God's throne with a fragrant aroma. So cool. It lends credibility to the TALK that we give if we provide the WALK to match it. The redeemed--*products of grace*--are now mirroring His grace through the sowing of seed. The message we believe has now become powerful and effective.

Finally, read the balance of the text and what you've started:

This service that you perform is NOT ONLY supplying the needs of God's people but is also overflowing in <u>many expressions of thanks to God.</u> BECAUSE of the service by which you have proved yourselves, <u>men will praise God</u> for the obedience that accompanies your confession of the gospel of Christ, and for your generosity in sharing with them and with everyone else. <u>And in their prayers for you</u> their hearts will go out to you, and because of the surpassing grace God has given you. Thanks be to God for His indescribable gift! (and for YOU, His inestimably valuable seed) (*2 Corinthians 9:12-15*) (emphasis mine)

proseed...

One Sunday, my son Bo was listening intently to my message, which is a source of great joy for me. In a conversation around the dinner table that afternoon, he suggested the title for this book. He is clever like that. He rattled off another play on words that I want to work with for a little. He said, "You've got to spiritualize your spiritual eyes." Here we go...

Visualization has a bad rap in some circles. Conservative Christians have perhaps overreacted to an exercise that was practiced somewhat in public schools. It sort of hinted at an Eastern meditation type practice that got some people (and justly so) concerned. The basic idea, however, is thoroughly sound, even Biblical. Abraham saw things that were not as though they were...and so forth. Indeed, vision is vital. It provides the road map from HERE to THERE. It certainly doesn't hurt to imagine your HARVEST as you plant your seed. The seed is the substance of things hoped for (nextpectancy). Vision is the offspring of core values. Those values determine our priorities, AND OUR PRIORITIES KEEP US ON TARGET. Our priorities enable the "restraints" that vision defines for us. *(Proverbs 29:18)*

But vision is only part of it. It is the first part, but

expectantseed 100

cannot stand alone.

Speaking of doing something, I've crossed several things off of my "Before I Die" list:

- Saw the Yankees at Yankee Stadium
- Toured Europe
- Visited the Taj Mahal
- Saw Willie Mays play centerfield
- Held public office
- Been scuba diving
- Been sky diving
- Rode home from previous event in an ambulance
- AND I'VE BEEN TO ISRAEL…(Special thanks to Marvin Hill)

Although many sites in the Holy Land are disputed, some are not. I know for a fact that I have walked where Jesus walked. One such place is the steep trail down the Mt. of Olives through Gethsemane to the Kidron Valley, across from the Eastern Gate into Old Jerusalem. Without question, I've experienced the same vista, looking south toward the Sinai, that Jesus shared with His disciples and that inspired one of the most familiar "seed" lessons of all. And here it is…

He replied, "Because you have so little faith. I tell you the truth, if you have faith as small as a mustard seed, you can say to this mountain, 'Move from here to there' and it will move. Nothing will be impossible for you." (Matthew 17:20)

From the trail I mentioned, you could see a place that was a modern marvel of engineering in Jesus' time. It was a symbol to Herod's wealth and power...and paranoia. It stood on a large hill that could be seen for miles. It is known as "The Herodian," and was the third largest palace in the world when Jesus saw it. In fact, He was born in the shadow of it in Bethlehem, three miles from the base of the fortress. While most mountains finish in a peak, this one is flat. Historians tell us that the earth moving accomplished by slaves was simply remarkable. They literally "moved a mountain" to provide a lavish retreat for Herod and his family. Was Jesus using this engineering marvel as a metaphor for what is possible to the believer? Was He philosophizing about the fleeting nature of a despot's power? (The palace now lies in ruins.) What is the point about a tiny bit of faith?

...and I wrote this in an email...

I wondered as I sat in church and listened to Pastors Chris and Stephen do a masterful job of leading the sanctuary class, how many of us wished that I would get past the seed thing? I do not sense that it has jelled for most of us yet. Some of you are having real revelations. You can appreciate now about our role and how much God values it. Still others, must be like the puppy in a famous Gary Trudeau cartoon. The caption read, "What a dog hears." The little bubble containing the words of the human suggested that the only thing the dog understood was his name. So it was, "Blah blah blah blah blah, SPOT... blah blah blah blah, SPOT!"

I feel like that dog sometimes. Every now and then I pick up on a word I understand--seed, sacrifice, harvest--but all the words in between are sometimes lost, misunderstood or forgotten. Jesus had twelve guys who, like me, were sometimes numb north of their shirt collar. Do you think that Andrew, James or John might have pinched a mustard seed between their thumbs and forefingers and started yelling at a mountain? Loving formulas, quick fixes and discipline-less deliverance. Might they have clinched the proverbial seed as they confessed loudly, "I BELIEVE, I BELIEVE, I BELIEVE" and then opened one eye to see if the mountain was gone yet? They didn't *get it*. I hope that we do, eventually. My EXPERIENCE has been that the mountain indeed moves. IT MUST. Nothing is impossible to us who believe. Sometimes, no EVERYTIME, it seems to take longer than I would like. But I am telling you, there are displaced mountains in my wake.

I am so used to it now, that I don't even think about it. Faith without works is dead and that means faith is more verb than noun. What I've learned, and expressed to my church family so many times, is that mountain-moving faith picks up a shovel and starts in. You have to heed the need...sow the seed...do the deed...feed the freed! No farmer ever harvested a crop by gripping a seed and hoping for harvest. I challenged you yesterday to visualize your harvest of righteousness. The VISION is critical. BUT IT IS NOT ENOUGH. If you have a vision BUT DON'T SOW THE SEED, YOU'RE JUST DAYDREAMING. The harvest CANNOT COME BEFORE THE SEED. The seed leads.

I've seen it work like this. I've got a mountain in front of me and a vision of relocation. SO I PICK UP A SHOVEL. Sure, I'm just one guy with one shovel, and WHAT IS THAT IN THE FACE OF SUCH AN OBSTACLE? Soon, Pastor Chris comes by and questions me. He is inspired by my commitment and runs home and gets his shovel. Pastor Stephen comes along and says, "I'll sing and play so that you guys can work in rhythm." Pastors Jimmy and Matt later join in because they want to be on a team that is getting something done. All this work is beginning to make a difference when finally a contractor shows up with platoons of workers and earth-moving equipment. BEFORE LONG THE MOUNTAIN IS GONE, because one person had a little bit of faith and heard that centuries old voice of God saying, "Just do it." Just do something.

NOBODY MOVED A MOUNTAIN BY SIMPLY WISHING IT WAS GONE, NOT EVEN IF HE OR SHE ADDED CHANTING TO THE MIX. You have to SOW the SEED.

This just in:

I mentioned earlier in this book about the vision our church had to build a school for three hundred children in Colombia, South America. I challenged the fellowship to pool their resources (seed) and we could accomplish amazing things, like building a school that clothes, feeds, and educates poor children. I've just returned from the site where our faith became sight. On Thanksgiving Day, 2006, we dedicated "La Escuela de la Semilla Preciosa" (The School of Precious Seed) in Ciénaga, Colombia, S.A.

In the service, we presented the school to the pastor and the denominational leadership in Colombia. That's right. We gave it away. The incredible family at UAG lived out, once again, what we have been saying through this book. You have to take your hands off of it--let it go-- and God will make sure to flow more resources through your hands because *HE IS GOING TO FUND THE HARVEST.*

I have one final thought as you proceed to be seed. I hope you will always wrestle with a question God asked me one morning while I was listening for Him. "If the only return on your seed were souls, would you still sow it? If there was no recognition, would you still offer acts of service? If no one saw or applauded, if it was not appreciated, would you still make a sacrifice?" I guess that sort of nails the motivation, doesn't it? The truth is, if it's all about money, we will never really understand this. Our *offense* will cloud our *revelation.* We cannot let that happen.

Cultivate the *nextpectation.*

Let go and let God do *what* and *how, when* and *where HE WILL.* Pray always for the wisdom to recognize it when it happens.

I closed my email series to the congregation with this:

"And if I should die, pull me around town behind my jeep with both of my hands sticking out of the coffin so that people will know that I didn't try to leave with any seed. AND, put a magnetic sign on the side of the hearse that reads, "You could be next."

Please let me hear from you.

bill@unitedassembly.com

Printed in the United States
77186LV00001B/13-108

9 781602 660717